Copyright © 2018 by In this Moment, LLC.
All rights reserved.
This book or any portion thereof may not be reproduced or used in any manner whatsoever without the expressed written permission of the publisher, except for the use of brief quotations in a book review.
Printed in the United States of America
First Printing, 2018
ISBN: 978-1-7329356-1-7
In this Moment, LLC
2519 N. McMullen Booth Road,
Suite 510, #112, Clearwater, FL 33761
www.inthismomentbooks.com

In this Moment™ is a registered trademark.

Table of Contents

Page	Age	Date
2-5		
6-9		
10-13		
14-17		
18-21		
22-25		
26-29		
30-33		
34-37		
38-41		
42-45		
46-49		

Page	Age	Date
50-53		
54-57		
58-61		
62-65		
66-69		
70-73		
74-77		
78-81		
82-85		
86-89		
90-93		
94-97		
98-101		
102-105		
106-109		
110-113		
114-117		
118-121		
122-125		
126-129		
130-133		
134-137		
138-141		

Year:_____ Age:_____

YEARLY REFLECTION

Since last year, my body has:_____
_____

Since last year, my heart has:_____
_____

Some of the things I've learned this year are:_____
_____

Some of the activities I've enjoyed this year are:_____
_____

Some of the people I've hung out with the most are:_____
_____

Some of the places I've really enjoyed this year are:_____
_____

Here are the year's top moments that I know will stay in my heart:_____
_____

When I think of the entire year, I would describe it as: _____
_____

IN THIS MOMENT

AROUND ME, I
See: _____
Hear: _____
Smell: _____
Taste: _____
Feel: _____

Overall, I would say that life is: _____

My heart is: _____

THE TOP THREE THOUGHTS THAT MAKE ME SMILE

1. _____
2. _____
3. _____

One piece of advice I'd give to people younger than me: _____
_____
_____

One piece of advice I'd give to people older than me: _____
_____
_____

If I could eat anything right now it would be: _____
_____
_____

If I could talk to anyone I would call: _____
_____
_____

If I could teleport anywhere I would go: _____
_____
_____

This is what I would do there: _____
_____
_____

If I could have one wish come true for me by my next birthday, it would be: _____
_____

Year:_____ Age:_____

YEARLY REFLECTION

Since last year, my body has:_____
_____

Since last year, my heart has:_____
_____

Some of the things I've learned this year are:_____
_____

Some of the activities I've enjoyed this year are:_____
_____

Some of the people I've hung out with the most are:_____
_____

Some of the places I've really enjoyed this year are:_____
_____

Here are the year's top moments that I know will stay in my heart:_____
_____

When I think of the entire year, I would describe it as: _____
_____

IN THIS MOMENT

AROUND ME, I

See: _____

Hear: _____

Smell: _____

Taste: _____

Feel: _____

Overall, I would say that life is: _____

My heart is: _____

THE TOP THREE THOUGHTS THAT MAKE ME SMILE

1. _____
2. _____
3. _____

One piece of advice I'd give to people younger than me:_____
_____
_____

One piece of advice I'd give to people older than me:_____
_____
_____

If I could eat anything right now it would be:_____
_____
_____

If I could talk to anyone I would call:_____
_____
_____

If I could teleport anywhere I would go:_____
_____
_____

This is what I would do there:_____
_____
_____

If I could have one wish come true for me by my next birthday, it would be:_____
_____
_____

Year:_____ Age:_____

YEARLY REFLECTION

Since last year, my body has:_____
_____

Since last year, my heart has:_____
_____

Some of the things I've learned this year are:_____
_____

Some of the activities I've enjoyed this year are:_____
_____

Some of the people I've hung out with the most are:_____
_____

Some of the places I've really enjoyed this year are:_____
_____

Here are the year's top moments that I know will stay in my heart:_____
_____

When I think of the entire year, I would describe it as: _____
_____

IN THIS MOMENT

AROUND ME, I

See: _____

Hear: _____

Smell: _____

Taste: _____

Feel: _____

Overall, I would say that life is: _____

My heart is: _____

THE TOP THREE THOUGHTS THAT MAKE ME SMILE

1. _____

2. _____

3. _____

One piece of advice I'd give to people younger than me: _____
_____
_____

One piece of advice I'd give to people older than me: _____
_____
_____

If I could eat anything right now it would be: _____
_____
_____

If I could talk to anyone I would call: _____
_____
_____

If I could teleport anywhere I would go: _____
_____
_____

This is what I would do there: _____
_____
_____

If I could have one wish come true for me by my next birthday, it would be: _____
_____

Year:_____   Age:_____

YEARLY REFLECTION

Since last year, my body has:_____
_____

Since last year, my heart has:_____
_____

Some of the things I've learned this year are:_____
_____

Some of the activities I've enjoyed this year are:_____
_____

Some of the people I've hung out with the most are:_____
_____

Some of the places I've really enjoyed this year are:_____
_____

Here are the year's top moments that I know will stay in my heart:_____
_____

When I think of the entire year, I would describe it as: _____
_____

IN THIS MOMENT

AROUND ME, I
See: _____
Hear: _____
Smell: _____
Taste: _____
Feel: _____

Overall, I would say that life is: _____

My heart is: _____

THE TOP THREE THOUGHTS THAT MAKE ME SMILE

1. _____
2. _____
3. _____

One piece of advice I'd give to people younger than me: _____
_____
_____

One piece of advice I'd give to people older than me: _____
_____
_____

If I could eat anything right now it would be: _____
_____
_____

If I could talk to anyone I would call: _____
_____
_____

If I could teleport anywhere I would go: _____
_____
_____

This is what I would do there: _____
_____
_____

If I could have one wish come true for me by my next birthday, it would be: _____
_____

Year:_____ Age:_____

YEARLY REFLECTION

Since last year, my body has:_____
_____

Since last year, my heart has:_____
_____

Some of the things I've learned this year are:_____
_____

Some of the activities I've enjoyed this year are:_____
_____

Some of the people I've hung out with the most are:_____
_____

Some of the places I've really enjoyed this year are:_____
_____

Here are the year's top moments that I know will stay in my heart:_____
_____

When I think of the entire year, I would describe it as: _____
_____

IN THIS MOMENT

AROUND ME, I

See: _____

Hear: _____

Smell: _____

Taste: _____

Feel: _____

Overall, I would say that life is: _____

My heart is: _____

THE TOP THREE THOUGHTS THAT MAKE ME SMILE

1. _____
2. _____
3. _____

One piece of advice I'd give to people younger than me: _____
_____
_____

One piece of advice I'd give to people older than me: _____
_____
_____

If I could eat anything right now it would be: _____
_____
_____

If I could talk to anyone I would call: _____
_____
_____

If I could teleport anywhere I would go: _____
_____
_____

This is what I would do there: _____
_____
_____

If I could have one wish come true for me by my next birthday, it would be: _____
_____

Year:_____ Age:_____

YEARLY REFLECTION

Since last year, my body has:_____
_____

Since last year, my heart has:_____
_____

Some of the things I've learned this year are:_____
_____

Some of the activities I've enjoyed this year are:_____
_____

Some of the people I've hung out with the most are:_____
_____

Some of the places I've really enjoyed this year are:_____
_____

Here are the year's top moments that I know will stay in my heart:_____
_____

When I think of the entire year, I would describe it as: _____
_____

IN THIS MOMENT

AROUND ME, I
See: _____
Hear: _____
Smell: _____
Taste: _____
Feel: _____

Overall, I would say that life is: _____

My heart is: _____

THE TOP THREE THOUGHTS THAT MAKE ME SMILE

1. _____
2. _____
3. _____

One piece of advice I'd give to people younger than me: _____
_____
_____

One piece of advice I'd give to people older than me: _____
_____
_____

If I could eat anything right now it would be: _____
_____
_____

If I could talk to anyone I would call: _____
_____
_____

If I could teleport anywhere I would go: _____
_____
_____

This is what I would do there: _____
_____
_____

If I could have one wish come true for me by my next birthday, it would be: _____
_____

Year:_____   Age:_____

YEARLY REFLECTION

Since last year, my body has:_____
_____

Since last year, my heart has:_____
_____

Some of the things I've learned this year are:_____
_____

Some of the activities I've enjoyed this year are:_____
_____

Some of the people I've hung out with the most are:_____
_____

Some of the places I've really enjoyed this year are:_____
_____

Here are the year's top moments that I know will stay in my heart:_____
_____

When I think of the entire year, I would describe it as: _____
_____

IN THIS MOMENT

AROUND ME, I
See: _____
Hear: _____
Smell: _____
Taste: _____
Feel: _____

Overall, I would say that life is: _____

My heart is: _____

THE TOP THREE THOUGHTS THAT MAKE ME SMILE

1. _____
2. _____
3. _____

One piece of advice I'd give to people younger than me: _____
_____
_____

One piece of advice I'd give to people older than me: _____
_____
_____

If I could eat anything right now it would be: _____
_____
_____

If I could talk to anyone I would call: _____
_____
_____

If I could teleport anywhere I would go: _____
_____
_____

This is what I would do there: _____
_____
_____

If I could have one wish come true for me by my next birthday, it would be: _____
_____
_____

Year: _____   Age: _____

YEARLY REFLECTION

Since last year, my body has: _____
_____

Since last year, my heart has: _____
_____

Some of the things I've learned this year are: _____
_____

Some of the activities I've enjoyed this year are: _____
_____

Some of the people I've hung out with the most are: _____
_____

Some of the places I've really enjoyed this year are: _____
_____

Here are the year's top moments that I know will stay in my heart: _____
_____

When I think of the entire year, I would describe it as: _____
_____

IN THIS MOMENT

AROUND ME, I
See: _____

Hear: _____

Smell: _____

Taste: _____

Feel: _____

Overall, I would say that life is: _____

My heart is: _____

THE TOP THREE THOUGHTS THAT MAKE ME SMILE

1. _____

2. _____

3. _____

One piece of advice I'd give to people younger than me: _____
_____
_____

One piece of advice I'd give to people older than me: _____
_____
_____

If I could eat anything right now it would be: _____
_____
_____

If I could talk to anyone I would call: _____
_____
_____

If I could teleport anywhere I would go: _____
_____
_____

This is what I would do there: _____
_____
_____

If I could have one wish come true for me by my next birthday, it would be: _____
_____

Year:_____   Age:_____

YEARLY REFLECTION

Since last year, my body has:_____
_____

Since last year, my heart has:_____
_____

Some of the things I've learned this year are:_____
_____

Some of the activities I've enjoyed this year are:_____
_____

Some of the people I've hung out with the most are:_____
_____

Some of the places I've really enjoyed this year are:_____
_____

Here are the year's top moments that I know will stay in my heart:_____
_____

When I think of the entire year, I would describe it as: _____
_____

IN THIS MOMENT

AROUND ME, I

See: _____

Hear: _____

Smell: _____

Taste: _____

Feel: _____

Overall, I would say that life is: _____

My heart is: _____

THE TOP THREE THOUGHTS THAT MAKE ME SMILE

1. _____

2. _____

3. _____

One piece of advice I'd give to people younger than me: _____
_____
_____

One piece of advice I'd give to people older than me: _____
_____
_____

If I could eat anything right now it would be: _____
_____
_____

If I could talk to anyone I would call: _____
_____
_____

If I could teleport anywhere I would go: _____
_____
_____

This is what I would do there: _____
_____
_____

If I could have one wish come true for me by my next birthday, it would be: _____
_____

Year:_____ Age:_____

YEARLY REFLECTION

Since last year, my body has:_____
_____

Since last year, my heart has:_____
_____

Some of the things I've learned this year are:_____
_____

Some of the activities I've enjoyed this year are:_____
_____

Some of the people I've hung out with the most are:_____
_____

Some of the places I've really enjoyed this year are:_____
_____

Here are the year's top moments that I know will stay in my heart:_____
_____

When I think of the entire year, I would describe it as: _____
_____

IN THIS MOMENT

AROUND ME, I
See: _____
Hear: _____
Smell: _____
Taste: _____
Feel: _____

Overall, I would say that life is: _____

My heart is: _____

THE TOP THREE THOUGHTS THAT MAKE ME SMILE

1. _____
2. _____
3. _____

One piece of advice I'd give to people younger than me: _____
_____
_____

One piece of advice I'd give to people older than me: _____
_____
_____

If I could eat anything right now it would be: _____
_____
_____

If I could talk to anyone I would call: _____
_____
_____

If I could teleport anywhere I would go: _____
_____
_____

This is what I would do there: _____
_____
_____

If I could have one wish come true for me by my next birthday, it would be: _____
_____

Year:_____   Age:_____

YEARLY REFLECTION

Since last year, my body has:_____
_____

Since last year, my heart has:_____
_____

Some of the things I've learned this year are:_____
_____

Some of the activities I've enjoyed this year are:_____
_____

Some of the people I've hung out with the most are:_____
_____

Some of the places I've really enjoyed this year are:_____
_____

Here are the year's top moments that I know will stay in my heart:_____
_____

When I think of the entire year, I would describe it as: _____
_____

IN THIS MOMENT

AROUND ME, I
See: _____
Hear: _____
Smell: _____
Taste: _____
Feel: _____

Overall, I would say that life is: _____

My heart is: _____

THE TOP THREE THOUGHTS THAT MAKE ME SMILE

1. _____
2. _____
3. _____

One piece of advice I'd give to people younger than me:_____
_____
_____

One piece of advice I'd give to people older than me:_____
_____
_____

If I could eat anything right now it would be:_____
_____
_____

If I could talk to anyone I would call:_____
_____
_____

If I could teleport anywhere I would go:_____
_____
_____

This is what I would do there:_____
_____
_____

If I could have one wish come true for me by my next birthday, it would be:_____
_____

Year:_____ Age:_____

YEARLY REFLECTION

Since last year, my body has:_____
_____

Since last year, my heart has:_____
_____

Some of the things I've learned this year are:_____
_____

Some of the activities I've enjoyed this year are:_____
_____

Some of the people I've hung out with the most are:_____
_____

Some of the places I've really enjoyed this year are:_____
_____

Here are the year's top moments that I know will stay in my heart:_____
_____

When I think of the entire year, I would describe it as: _____
_____

IN THIS MOMENT

AROUND ME, I
See: _____

Hear: _____

Smell: _____

Taste: _____

Feel: _____

Overall, I would say that life is: _____

My heart is: _____

THE TOP THREE THOUGHTS THAT MAKE ME SMILE

1. _____
2. _____
3. _____

One piece of advice I'd give to people younger than me: _____
_____
_____

One piece of advice I'd give to people older than me: _____
_____
_____

If I could eat anything right now it would be: _____
_____
_____

If I could talk to anyone I would call: _____
_____
_____

If I could teleport anywhere I would go: _____
_____
_____

This is what I would do there: _____
_____
_____

If I could have one wish come true for me by my next birthday, it would be: _____
_____

Year:_____   Age:_____

YEARLY REFLECTION

Since last year, my body has:_____
_____

Since last year, my heart has:_____
_____

Some of the things I've learned this year are:_____
_____

Some of the activities I've enjoyed this year are:_____
_____

Some of the people I've hung out with the most are:_____
_____

Some of the places I've really enjoyed this year are:_____
_____

Here are the year's top moments that I know will stay in my heart:_____
_____

When I think of the entire year, I would describe it as: _____
_____

IN THIS MOMENT

AROUND ME, I
See: _____

Hear: _____

Smell: _____

Taste: _____

Feel: _____

Overall, I would say that life is: _____

My heart is: _____

THE TOP THREE THOUGHTS THAT MAKE ME SMILE

1. _____

2. _____

3. _____

One piece of advice I'd give to people younger than me: _____
_____
_____

One piece of advice I'd give to people older than me: _____
_____
_____

If I could eat anything right now it would be: _____
_____
_____

If I could talk to anyone I would call: _____
_____
_____

If I could teleport anywhere I would go: _____
_____
_____

This is what I would do there: _____
_____
_____

If I could have one wish come true for me by my next birthday, it would be: _____
_____

Year:_____   Age:_____

YEARLY REFLECTION

Since last year, my body has:_____
_____

Since last year, my heart has:_____
_____

Some of the things I've learned this year are:_____
_____

Some of the activities I've enjoyed this year are:_____
_____

Some of the people I've hung out with the most are:_____
_____

Some of the places I've really enjoyed this year are:_____
_____

Here are the year's top moments that I know will stay in my heart:_____
_____

When I think of the entire year, I would describe it as: _____
_____

IN THIS MOMENT

AROUND ME, I
See: _____

Hear: _____

Smell: _____

Taste: _____

Feel: _____

Overall, I would say that life is: _____

My heart is: _____

THE TOP THREE THOUGHTS THAT MAKE ME SMILE

1. _____

2. _____

3. _____

One piece of advice I'd give to people younger than me: _____
_____
_____

One piece of advice I'd give to people older than me: _____
_____
_____

If I could eat anything right now it would be: _____
_____
_____

If I could talk to anyone I would call: _____
_____
_____

If I could teleport anywhere I would go: _____
_____
_____

This is what I would do there: _____
_____
_____

If I could have one wish come true for me by my next birthday, it would be: _____
_____

Year:_____   Age:_____

YEARLY REFLECTION

Since last year, my body has:_____
_____

Since last year, my heart has:_____
_____

Some of the things I've learned this year are:_____
_____

Some of the activities I've enjoyed this year are:_____
_____

Some of the people I've hung out with the most are:_____
_____

Some of the places I've really enjoyed this year are:_____
_____

Here are the year's top moments that I know will stay in my heart:_____
_____

When I think of the entire year, I would describe it as: _____
_____

IN THIS MOMENT

AROUND ME, I

See: _____

Hear: _____

Smell: _____

Taste: _____

Feel: _____

Overall, I would say that life is: _____

My heart is: _____

THE TOP THREE THOUGHTS THAT MAKE ME SMILE

1. _____

2. _____

3. _____

One piece of advice I'd give to people younger than me: _____
_____
_____

One piece of advice I'd give to people older than me: _____
_____
_____

If I could eat anything right now it would be: _____
_____
_____

If I could talk to anyone I would call: _____
_____
_____

If I could teleport anywhere I would go: _____
_____
_____

This is what I would do there: _____
_____
_____

If I could have one wish come true for me by my next birthday, it would be: _____
_____

Year:_____   Age:_____

YEARLY REFLECTION

Since last year, my body has:_____
_____

Since last year, my heart has:_____
_____

Some of the things I've learned this year are:_____
_____

Some of the activities I've enjoyed this year are:_____
_____

Some of the people I've hung out with the most are:_____
_____

Some of the places I've really enjoyed this year are:_____
_____

Here are the year's top moments that I know will stay in my heart:____
_____

When I think of the entire year, I would describe it as: _____
_____

IN THIS MOMENT

AROUND ME, I

See: _____

Hear: _____

Smell: _____

Taste: _____

Feel: _____

Overall, I would say that life is: _____

My heart is: _____

THE TOP THREE THOUGHTS THAT MAKE ME SMILE

1. _____
2. _____
3. _____

One piece of advice I'd give to people younger than me: _____
_____
_____

One piece of advice I'd give to people older than me: _____
_____
_____

If I could eat anything right now it would be: _____
_____
_____

If I could talk to anyone I would call: _____
_____
_____

If I could teleport anywhere I would go: _____
_____
_____

This is what I would do there: _____
_____
_____

If I could have one wish come true for me by my next birthday, it would be: _____
_____
_____

Year:_____   Age:_____

YEARLY REFLECTION

Since last year, my body has:_____
_____

Since last year, my heart has:_____
_____

Some of the things I've learned this year are:_____
_____

Some of the activities I've enjoyed this year are:_____
_____

Some of the people I've hung out with the most are:_____
_____

Some of the places I've really enjoyed this year are:_____
_____

Here are the year's top moments that I know will stay in my heart:_____
_____

When I think of the entire year, I would describe it as: _____
_____

IN THIS MOMENT

AROUND ME, I
See: _____

Hear: _____

Smell: _____

Taste: _____

Feel: _____

Overall, I would say that life is: _____

My heart is: _____

THE TOP THREE THOUGHTS THAT MAKE ME SMILE

1. _____
2. _____
3. _____

One piece of advice I'd give to people younger than me: _____
_____
_____

One piece of advice I'd give to people older than me: _____
_____
_____

If I could eat anything right now it would be: _____
_____
_____

If I could talk to anyone I would call: _____
_____
_____

If I could teleport anywhere I would go: _____
_____
_____

This is what I would do there: _____
_____
_____

If I could have one wish come true for me by my next birthday, it would be: _____
_____

Year:_____ Age:_____

YEARLY REFLECTION

Since last year, my body has:_____
_____

Since last year, my heart has:_____
_____

Some of the things I've learned this year are:_____
_____

Some of the activities I've enjoyed this year are:_____
_____

Some of the people I've hung out with the most are:_____
_____

Some of the places I've really enjoyed this year are:_____
_____

Here are the year's top moments that I know will stay in my heart:_____
_____

When I think of the entire year, I would describe it as: _____
_____

IN THIS MOMENT

AROUND ME, I
See: _____

Hear: _____

Smell: _____

Taste: _____

Feel: _____

Overall, I would say that life is: _____

My heart is: _____

THE TOP THREE THOUGHTS THAT MAKE ME SMILE

1. _____
2. _____
3. _____

One piece of advice I'd give to people younger than me: _____
_____
_____

One piece of advice I'd give to people older than me: _____
_____
_____

If I could eat anything right now it would be: _____
_____
_____

If I could talk to anyone I would call: _____
_____
_____

If I could teleport anywhere I would go: _____
_____
_____

This is what I would do there: _____
_____
_____

If I could have one wish come true for me by my next birthday, it would be: _____
_____

Year:_____   Age:_____

YEARLY REFLECTION

Since last year, my body has:_____
_____

Since last year, my heart has:_____
_____

Some of the things I've learned this year are:_____
_____

Some of the activities I've enjoyed this year are:_____
_____

Some of the people I've hung out with the most are:_____
_____

Some of the places I've really enjoyed this year are:_____
_____

Here are the year's top moments that I know will stay in my heart:_____
_____

When I think of the entire year, I would describe it as: _____
_____

IN THIS MOMENT

AROUND ME, I

See: _____

Hear: _____

Smell: _____

Taste: _____

Feel: _____

Overall, I would say that life is: _____

My heart is: _____

THE TOP THREE THOUGHTS THAT MAKE ME SMILE

1. _____

2. _____

3. _____

One piece of advice I'd give to people younger than me: _____
_____
_____

One piece of advice I'd give to people older than me: _____
_____
_____

If I could eat anything right now it would be: _____
_____
_____

If I could talk to anyone I would call: _____
_____
_____

If I could teleport anywhere I would go: _____
_____
_____

This is what I would do there: _____
_____
_____

If I could have one wish come true for me by my next birthday, it would be: _____
_____

Year:_____ Age:_____

YEARLY REFLECTION

Since last year, my body has:_____
_____

Since last year, my heart has:_____
_____

Some of the things I've learned this year are:_____
_____

Some of the activities I've enjoyed this year are:_____
_____

Some of the people I've hung out with the most are:_____
_____

Some of the places I've really enjoyed this year are:_____
_____

Here are the year's top moments that I know will stay in my heart:_____
_____

When I think of the entire year, I would describe it as: _____
_____

IN THIS MOMENT

AROUND ME, I
See: _____

Hear: _____

Smell: _____

Taste: _____

Feel: _____

Overall, I would say that life is: _____

My heart is: _____

THE TOP THREE THOUGHTS THAT MAKE ME SMILE

1. _____
2. _____
3. _____

One piece of advice I'd give to people younger than me: _____
_____
_____

One piece of advice I'd give to people older than me: _____
_____
_____

If I could eat anything right now it would be: _____
_____
_____

If I could talk to anyone I would call: _____
_____
_____

If I could teleport anywhere I would go: _____
_____
_____

This is what I would do there: _____
_____
_____

If I could have one wish come true for me by my next birthday, it would be: _____
_____

Year:_____ Age:_____

YEARLY REFLECTION

Since last year, my body has:_____
_____

Since last year, my heart has:_____
_____

Some of the things I've learned this year are:_____
_____

Some of the activities I've enjoyed this year are:_____
_____

Some of the people I've hung out with the most are:_____
_____

Some of the places I've really enjoyed this year are:_____
_____

Here are the year's top moments that I know will stay in my heart:_____
_____

When I think of the entire year, I would describe it as: _____
_____

IN THIS MOMENT

AROUND ME, I

See: _____

Hear: _____

Smell: _____

Taste: _____

Feel: _____

Overall, I would say that life is: _____

My heart is: _____

THE TOP THREE THOUGHTS THAT MAKE ME SMILE

1. _____

2. _____

3. _____

One piece of advice I'd give to people younger than me: _____
_____
_____

One piece of advice I'd give to people older than me: _____
_____
_____

If I could eat anything right now it would be: _____
_____
_____

If I could talk to anyone I would call: _____
_____

If I could teleport anywhere I would go: _____
_____
_____

This is what I would do there: _____
_____
_____

If I could have one wish come true for me by my next birthday, it would be: _____
_____

Year:_____   Age:_____

YEARLY REFLECTION

Since last year, my body has:_____
_____

Since last year, my heart has:_____
_____

Some of the things I've learned this year are:_____
_____

Some of the activities I've enjoyed this year are:_____
_____

Some of the people I've hung out with the most are:_____
_____

Some of the places I've really enjoyed this year are:_____
_____

Here are the year's top moments that I know will stay in my heart:_____
_____

When I think of the entire year, I would describe it as: _____
_____

IN THIS MOMENT

AROUND ME, I

See: _____

Hear: _____

Smell: _____

Taste: _____

Feel: _____

Overall, I would say that life is: _____

My heart is: _____

THE TOP THREE THOUGHTS THAT MAKE ME SMILE

1. _____
2. _____
3. _____

One piece of advice I'd give to people younger than me: _____
_____
_____

One piece of advice I'd give to people older than me: _____
_____
_____

If I could eat anything right now it would be: _____
_____
_____

If I could talk to anyone I would call: _____
_____
_____

If I could teleport anywhere I would go: _____
_____
_____

This is what I would do there: _____
_____
_____

If I could have one wish come true for me by my next birthday, it would be: _____
_____

Year:_____ Age:_____

YEARLY REFLECTION

Since last year, my body has:_____
_____

Since last year, my heart has:_____
_____

Some of the things I've learned this year are:_____
_____

Some of the activities I've enjoyed this year are:_____
_____

Some of the people I've hung out with the most are:_____
_____

Some of the places I've really enjoyed this year are:_____
_____

Here are the year's top moments that I know will stay in my heart:_____
_____

When I think of the entire year, I would describe it as: _____
_____

IN THIS MOMENT

AROUND ME, I
See: _____
Hear: _____
Smell: _____
Taste: _____
Feel: _____

Overall, I would say that life is: _____

My heart is: _____

THE TOP THREE THOUGHTS THAT MAKE ME SMILE

1. _____
2. _____
3. _____

One piece of advice I'd give to people younger than me: _____
_____
_____

One piece of advice I'd give to people older than me: _____
_____
_____

If I could eat anything right now it would be: _____
_____
_____

If I could talk to anyone I would call: _____
_____
_____

If I could teleport anywhere I would go: _____
_____
_____

This is what I would do there: _____
_____
_____

If I could have one wish come true for me by my next birthday, it would be: _____
_____

Year:_____   Age:_____

YEARLY REFLECTION

Since last year, my body has:_____
_____

Since last year, my heart has:_____
_____

Some of the things I've learned this year are:_____
_____

Some of the activities I've enjoyed this year are:_____
_____

Some of the people I've hung out with the most are:_____
_____

Some of the places I've really enjoyed this year are:_____
_____

Here are the year's top moments that I know will stay in my heart:_____
_____

When I think of the entire year, I would describe it as: _____
_____

IN THIS MOMENT

AROUND ME, I

See: _____

Hear: _____

Smell: _____

Taste: _____

Feel: _____

Overall, I would say that life is: _____

My heart is: _____

THE TOP THREE THOUGHTS THAT MAKE ME SMILE

1. _____

2. _____

3. _____

One piece of advice I'd give to people younger than me: _____
_____
_____

One piece of advice I'd give to people older than me: _____
_____
_____

If I could eat anything right now it would be _____
_____
_____

If I could talk to anyone I would call: _____
_____
_____

If I could teleport anywhere I would go: _____
_____
_____

This is what I would do there: _____
_____
_____

If I could have one wish come true for me by my next birthday, it would be: _____
_____

Year:_____ Age:_____

YEARLY REFLECTION

Since last year, my body has:_____
_____

Since last year, my heart has:_____
_____

Some of the things I've learned this year are:_____
_____

Some of the activities I've enjoyed this year are:_____
_____

Some of the people I've hung out with the most are:_____
_____

Some of the places I've really enjoyed this year are:_____
_____

Here are the year's top moments that I know will stay in my heart:_____
_____

When I think of the entire year, I would describe it as: _____
_____

IN THIS MOMENT

AROUND ME, I
See: _____
Hear: _____
Smell: _____
Taste: _____
Feel: _____

Overall, I would say that life is: _____

My heart is: _____

THE TOP THREE THOUGHTS THAT MAKE ME SMILE

1. _____
2. _____
3. _____

One piece of advice I'd give to people younger than me: _____
_____
_____

One piece of advice I'd give to people older than me: _____
_____
_____

If I could eat anything right now it would be: _____
_____
_____

If I could talk to anyone I would call: _____
_____
_____

If I could teleport anywhere I would go: _____
_____
_____

This is what I would do there: _____
_____
_____

If I could have one wish come true for me by my next birthday, it would be: _____
_____

Year:_____ Age:_____

YEARLY REFLECTION

Since last year, my body has:_____
_____

Since last year, my heart has:_____
_____

Some of the things I've learned this year are:_____
_____

Some of the activities I've enjoyed this year are:_____
_____

Some of the people I've hung out with the most are:_____
_____

Some of the places I've really enjoyed this year are:_____
_____

Here are the year's top moments that I know will stay in my heart:_____
_____

When I think of the entire year, I would describe it as: _____
_____

IN THIS MOMENT

AROUND ME, I
See: _____
Hear: _____
Smell: _____
Taste: _____
Feel: _____

Overall, I would say that life is: _____

My heart is: _____

THE TOP THREE THOUGHTS THAT MAKE ME SMILE

1. _____
2. _____
3. _____

One piece of advice I'd give to people younger than me: _____
_____
_____

One piece of advice I'd give to people older than me: _____
_____
_____

If I could eat anything right now it would be: _____
_____
_____

If I could talk to anyone I would call: _____
_____
_____

If I could teleport anywhere I would go: _____
_____
_____

This is what I would do there: _____
_____
_____

If I could have one wish come true for me by my next birthday, it would be: _____
_____

Year:_____   Age:_____

YEARLY REFLECTION

Since last year, my body has:_____
_____

Since last year, my heart has:_____
_____

Some of the things I've learned this year are:_____
_____

Some of the activities I've enjoyed this year are:_____
_____

Some of the people I've hung out with the most are:_____
_____

Some of the places I've really enjoyed this year are:_____
_____

Here are the year's top moments that I know will stay in my heart:_____
_____

When I think of the entire year, I would describe it as: _____

IN THIS MOMENT

AROUND ME, I

See: _____

Hear: _____

Smell: _____

Taste: _____

Feel: _____

Overall, I would say that life is: _____

My heart is: _____

THE TOP THREE THOUGHTS THAT MAKE ME SMILE

1. _____
2. _____
3. _____

One piece of advice I'd give to people younger than me: _____
_____
_____

One piece of advice I'd give to people older than me: _____
_____
_____

If I could eat anything right now it would be: _____
_____
_____

If I could talk to anyone I would call: _____
_____
_____

If I could teleport anywhere I would go: _____
_____
_____

This is what I would do there: _____
_____
_____
_____

If I could have one wish come true for me by my next birthday, it would be: _____
_____

Year:_____ Age:_____

YEARLY REFLECTION

Since last year, my body has:_____
_____

Since last year, my heart has:_____
_____

Some of the things I've learned this year are:_____
_____

Some of the activities I've enjoyed this year are:_____
_____

Some of the people I've hung out with the most are:_____
_____

Some of the places I've really enjoyed this year are:_____
_____

Here are the year's top moments that I know will stay in my heart:_____
_____

When I think of the entire year, I would describe it as: _____
_____

IN THIS MOMENT

AROUND ME, I

See: _____

Hear: _____

Smell: _____

Taste: _____

Feel: _____

Overall, I would say that life is: _____

My heart is: _____

THE TOP THREE THOUGHTS THAT MAKE ME SMILE

1. _____
2. _____
3. _____

One piece of advice I'd give to people younger than me: _____
_____
_____

One piece of advice I'd give to people older than me: _____
_____
_____

If I could eat anything right now it would be: _____
_____
_____

If I could talk to anyone I would call: _____
_____
_____

If I could teleport anywhere I would go: _____
_____
_____

This is what I would do there: _____
_____
_____

If I could have one wish come true for me by my next birthday, it would be: _____
_____

Year:_____   Age:_____

YEARLY REFLECTION

Since last year, my body has:_____
_____

Since last year, my heart has:_____
_____

Some of the things I've learned this year are:_____
_____

Some of the activities I've enjoyed this year are:_____
_____

Some of the people I've hung out with the most are:_____
_____

Some of the places I've really enjoyed this year are:_____
_____

Here are the year's top moments that I know will stay in my heart:_____
_____

When I think of the entire year, I would describe it as: _____
_____

IN THIS MOMENT

AROUND ME, I

See: _____

Hear: _____

Smell: _____

Taste: _____

Feel: _____

Overall, I would say that life is: _____

My heart is: _____

THE TOP THREE THOUGHTS THAT MAKE ME SMILE

1. _____
2. _____
3. _____

One piece of advice I'd give to people younger than me: _____
_____
_____

One piece of advice I'd give to people older than me: _____
_____
_____

If I could eat anything right now it would be: _____
_____
_____

If I could talk to anyone I would call: _____
_____
_____

If I could teleport anywhere I would go: _____
_____
_____

This is what I would do there: _____
_____
_____

If I could have one wish come true for me by my next birthday, it would be: _____
_____

Year:_____   Age:_____

YEARLY REFLECTION

Since last year, my body has:_____
_____

Since last year, my heart has:_____
_____

Some of the things I've learned this year are:_____
_____

Some of the activities I've enjoyed this year are:_____
_____

Some of the people I've hung out with the most are:_____
_____

Some of the places I've really enjoyed this year are:_____
_____

Here are the year's top moments that I know will stay in my heart:_____
_____

When I think of the entire year, I would describe it as: _____
_____

IN THIS MOMENT

AROUND ME, I
See: _____
Hear: _____
Smell: _____
Taste: _____
Feel: _____

Overall, I would say that life is: _____

My heart is: _____

THE TOP THREE THOUGHTS THAT MAKE ME SMILE

1. _____
2. _____
3. _____

One piece of advice I'd give to people younger than me: _____
_____
_____

One piece of advice I'd give to people older than me: _____
_____
_____

If I could eat anything right now it would be: _____
_____
_____

If I could talk to anyone I would call: _____
_____
_____

If I could teleport anywhere I would go: _____
_____
_____

This is what I would do there: _____
_____
_____

If I could have one wish come true for me by my next birthday, it would be: _____
_____

Year:_____   Age:_____

YEARLY REFLECTION

Since last year, my body has:_____
_____

Since last year, my heart has:_____
_____

Some of the things I've learned this year are:_____
_____

Some of the activities I've enjoyed this year are:_____
_____

Some of the people I've hung out with the most are:_____
_____

Some of the places I've really enjoyed this year are:_____
_____

Here are the year's top moments that I know will stay in my heart:_____
_____

When I think of the entire year, I would describe it as:_____
_____

IN THIS MOMENT

AROUND ME, I
See: _____
Hear: _____
Smell: _____
Taste: _____
Feel: _____

Overall, I would say that life is: _____

My heart is: _____

THE TOP THREE THOUGHTS THAT MAKE ME SMILE

1. _____
2. _____
3. _____

One piece of advice I'd give to people younger than me: _____
_____
_____

One piece of advice I'd give to people older than me: _____
_____
_____

If I could eat anything right now it would be: _____
_____
_____

If I could talk to anyone I would call: _____
_____
_____

If I could teleport anywhere I would go: _____
_____
_____

This is what I would do there: _____
_____
_____

If I could have one wish come true for me by my next birthday, it would be: _____
_____
_____

Year:_____ Age:_____

YEARLY REFLECTION

Since last year, my body has: _____
_____

Since last year, my heart has: _____
_____

Some of the things I've learned this year are: _____
_____

Some of the activities I've enjoyed this year are: _____
_____

Some of the people I've hung out with the most are: _____
_____

Some of the places I've really enjoyed this year are: _____
_____

Here are the year's top moments that I know will stay in my heart: _____
_____

When I think of the entire year, I would describe it as: _____
_____

IN THIS MOMENT

AROUND ME, I
See: _____

Hear: _____

Smell: _____

Taste: _____

Feel: _____

Overall, I would say that life is: _____

My heart is: _____

THE TOP THREE THOUGHTS THAT MAKE ME SMILE

1. _____
2. _____
3. _____

One piece of advice I'd give to people younger than me: _____
_____
_____

One piece of advice I'd give to people older than me: _____
_____
_____

If I could eat anything right now it would be: _____
_____
_____

If I could talk to anyone I would call: _____
_____
_____

If I could teleport anywhere I would go: _____
_____
_____

This is what I would do there: _____
_____
_____

If I could have one wish come true for me by my next birthday, it would be: _____
_____
_____

HERE'S A PICTURE OF ME ON THIS BIRTHDAY...

Year:_____   Age:_____

YEARLY REFLECTION

Since last year, my body has:_____
_____

Since last year, my heart has:_____
_____

Some of the things I've learned this year are:_____
_____

Some of the activities I've enjoyed this year are:_____
_____

Some of the people I've hung out with the most are:_____
_____

Some of the places I've really enjoyed this year are:_____
_____

Here are the year's top moments that I know will stay in my heart:_____
_____

When I think of the entire year, I would describe it as: _____
_____

IN THIS MOMENT

AROUND ME, I
- See: _____
- Hear: _____
- Smell: _____
- Taste: _____
- Feel: _____

Overall, I would say that life is: _____

My heart is: _____

THE TOP THREE THOUGHTS THAT MAKE ME SMILE

1. _____
2. _____
3. _____

One piece of advice I'd give to people younger than me: _____
_____
_____

One piece of advice I'd give to people older than me: _____
_____
_____

If I could eat anything right now it would be: _____
_____
_____

If I could talk to anyone I would call: _____
_____
_____

If I could teleport anywhere I would go: _____
_____
_____

This is what I would do there: _____
_____
_____

If I could have one wish come true for me by my next birthday, it would be: _____
_____

HERE'S A PICTURE OF ME ON THIS BIRTHDAY...

Year:_____   Age:_____

YEARLY REFLECTION

Since last year, my body has:_____
_____

Since last year, my heart has:_____
_____

Some of the things I've learned this year are:_____
_____

Some of the activities I've enjoyed this year are:_____
_____

Some of the people I've hung out with the most are:_____
_____

Some of the places I've really enjoyed this year are:_____
_____

Here are the year's top moments that I know will stay in my heart:_____
_____

When I think of the entire year, I would describe it as: _____
_____

One piece of advice I'd give to people younger than me: _____
_____
_____

One piece of advice I'd give to people older than me: _____
_____
_____

If I could eat anything right now it would be: _____
_____
_____

If I could talk to anyone I would call: _____
_____
_____

If I could teleport anywhere I would go: _____
_____
_____

This is what I would do there: _____
_____
_____

If I could have one wish come true for me by my next birthday, it would
be: _____
_____

Year:_____   Age:_____

YEARLY REFLECTION

Since last year, my body has:_____
_____

Since last year, my heart has:_____
_____

Some of the things I've learned this year are:_____
_____

Some of the activities I've enjoyed this year are:_____
_____

Some of the people I've hung out with the most are:_____
_____

Some of the places I've really enjoyed this year are:_____
_____

Here are the year's top moments that I know will stay in my heart:_____
_____

When I think of the entire year, I would describe it as:_____
_____

IN THIS MOMENT

AROUND ME, I

See: _____

Hear: _____

Smell: _____

Taste: _____

Feel: _____

Overall, I would say that life is: _____

My heart is: _____

THE TOP THREE THOUGHTS THAT MAKE ME SMILE

1. _____
2. _____
3. _____

One piece of advice I'd give to people younger than me: _____

One piece of advice I'd give to people older than me: _____

If I could eat anything right now it would be: _____

If I could talk to anyone I would call: _____

If I could teleport anywhere I would go: _____

This is what I would do there: _____

If I could have one wish come true for me by my next birthday, it would be: _____